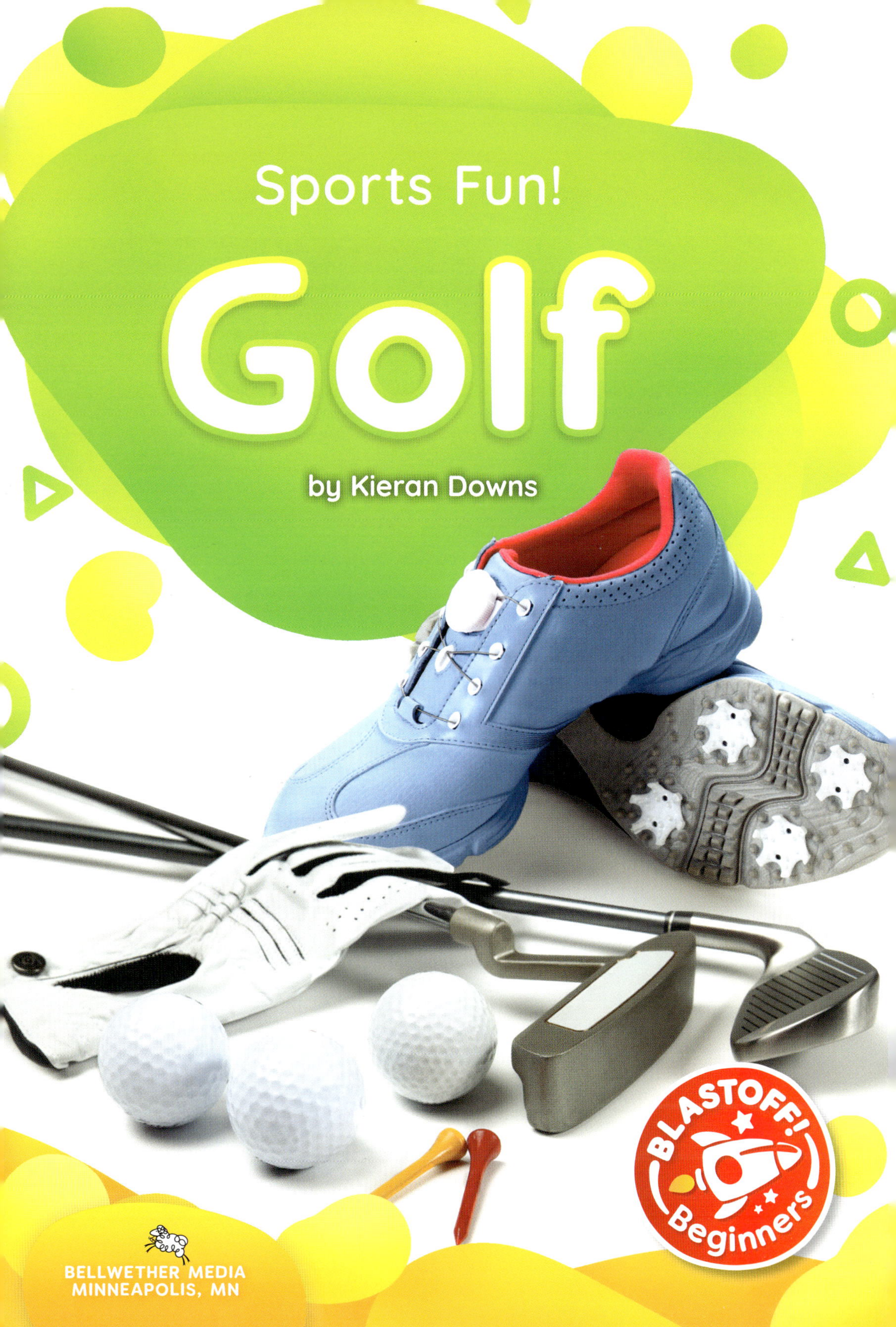
Sports Fun!
Golf
by Kieran Downs
BLASTOFF! Beginners
BELLWETHER MEDIA
MINNEAPOLIS, MN

Blastoff! Beginners are developed by literacy experts and educators to meet the needs of early readers. These engaging informational texts support young children as they begin reading about their world. Through simple language and high frequency words paired with crisp, colorful photos, Blastoff! Beginners launch young readers into the universe of independent reading.

Sight Words in This Book

an	into	some	to
for	is	the	use
get	it	their	with
have	on	they	your
he	play	this	
in	she	time	

This edition first published in 2024 by Bellwether Media, Inc.

Library of Congress Cataloging-in-Publication Data

Names: Downs, Kieran, author.
Title: Golf / by Kieran Downs.
Description: Minneapolis, MN : Bellwether Media, 2024. | Series: Blastoff! beginners. Sports fun! | Includes bibliographical references and index. | Audience: Ages 4-7 | Audience: Grades K-1
Identifiers: LCCN 2023035181 (print) | LCCN 2023035182 (ebook) | ISBN 9798886877670 (library binding) | ISBN 9798886878615 (ebook)
Subjects: LCSH: Golf--Juvenile literature.
Classification: LCC GV968 .D68 2024 (print) | LCC GV968 (ebook) | DDC 796.352--dc23/eng/20230807
LC record available at https://lccn.loc.gov/2023035181
LC ebook record available at https://lccn.loc.gov/2023035182

Editor: Christina Leaf Designer: Gabriel Hilger

Printed in the United States of America, North Mankato, MN.

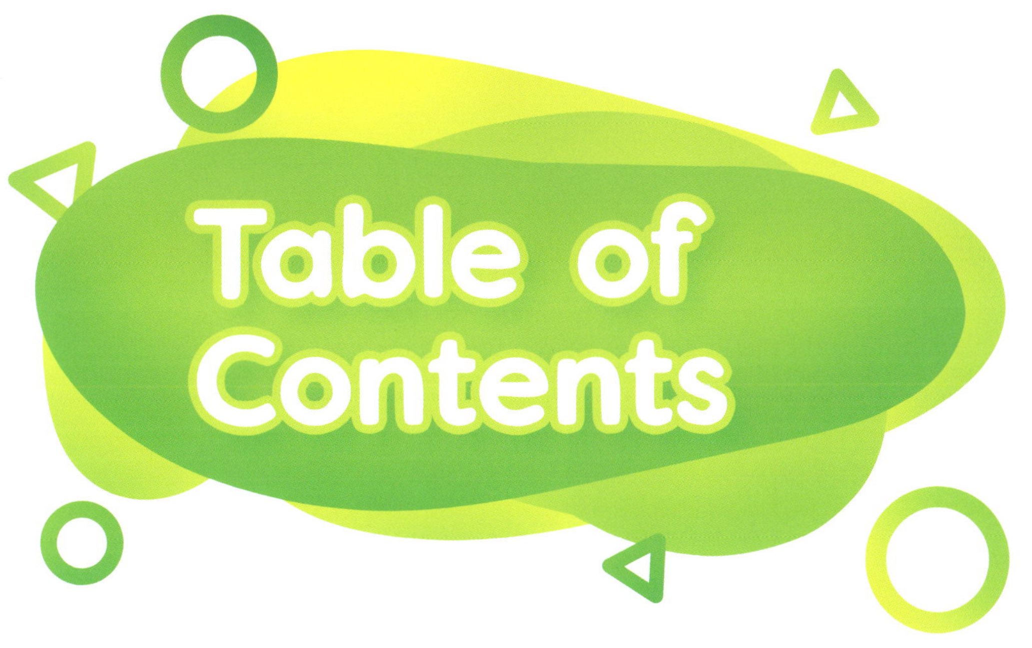

Table of Contents

Golf Time! 4
What Is Golf? 6
On the Course 10
Golf Facts 22
Glossary 23
To Learn More 24
Index 24

Get your clubs.
It is time for golf!

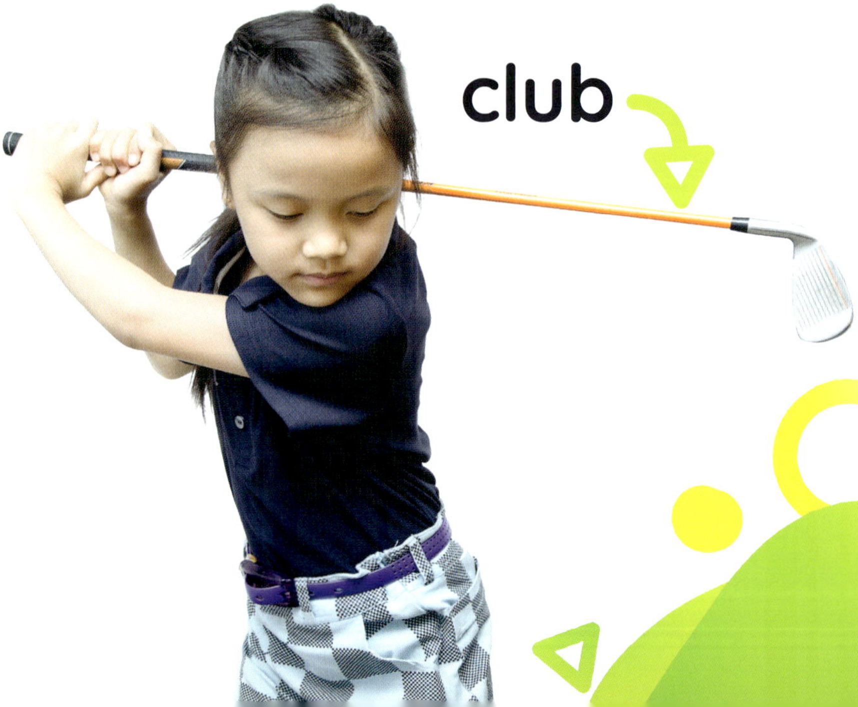

club

What Is Golf?

Golf is
an outdoor sport.
Golfers hit balls
into holes.

golf ball

Some golfers play on teams. Some play on their own.

team

On the Course

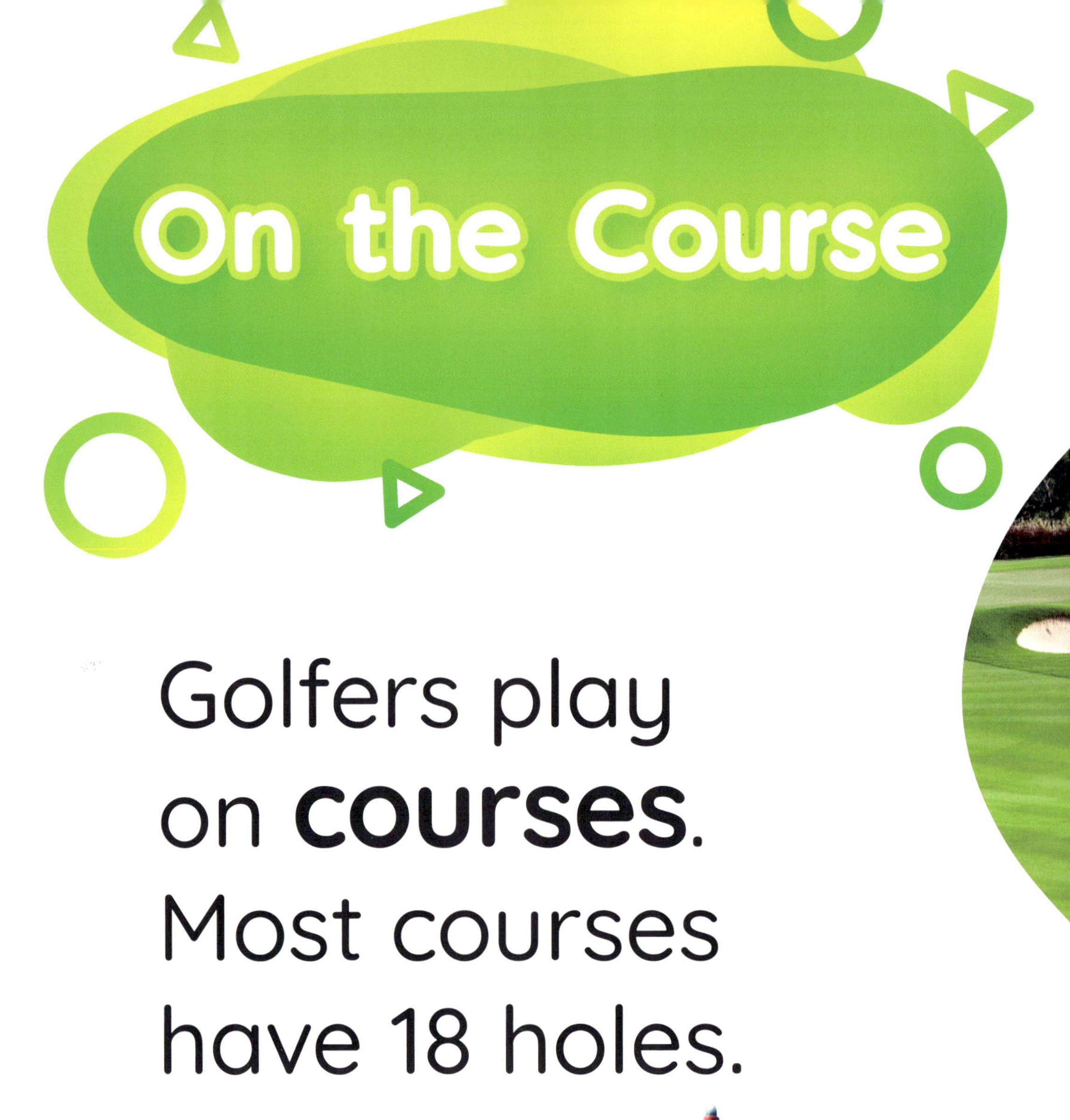

Golfers play on **courses**. Most courses have 18 holes.

course

Golfers use clubs to hit balls.

PUMA

They hit the ball
into the hole.
The fewest
hits wins!

hole

Golfers start
with **drives**.
The ball goes far!

driving

This golfer
is in sand.
She **chips**
the ball.

chipping

This golfer is near the hole. He **putts** the ball in!

putting

Golf Facts

Playing Golf

Golf Moves

drive chip putt

Glossary

chips

hits the ball so it goes high in the air

courses

grassy areas where golf is played

drives

hard hits that send the ball far

putts

carefully hits a golf ball into the hole

To Learn More

ON THE WEB

FACTSURFER

Factsurfer.com gives you a safe, fun way to find more information.

1. Go to www.factsurfer.com.
2. Enter "golf" into the search box and click 🔍.
3. Select your book cover to see a list of related content.

Index

balls, 6, 12, 14, 16, 18, 20
chips, 18, 19
clubs, 4, 12
courses, 10, 11
drives, 16, 17
golfers, 6, 8, 10, 12, 16, 18, 20
hit, 6, 12, 14
holes, 6, 10, 14, 15, 20
outdoor, 6
play, 8, 10
putts, 20, 21
sand, 18
teams, 8, 9
wins, 14

The images in this book are reproduced through the courtesy of: choja, cover, p. 1 (clubs, gloves, balls); studiocasper, cover, p. 1 (shoes); Mike Flippo, p. 3; Littlekidmoment, p. 4; SDI Productions, pp. 4-5; Valentina Proskurina, p. 6; Dasha Petrenko, pp. 6-7; kali9, pp. 8-9; romakoma, p. 10; 46design, pp. 10-11; Dan Thornberg, p. 12; JuanaNunez, pp. 12-13; Gregory Johnston, pp. 14-15; kamira777, pp. 16-17; NotarYES, pp. 18-19; MichaelSvoboda, pp. 20-21, 22 (playing golf); Olimpik, pp. 22, (drive), 23 (drives); Suchan, p. 22 (putt); Phil's Mommy, p. 23 (chips); goldenjack, p. 23 (courses); sonya etchison, p. 23 (putts).